Knights & Castles

PICTURE THAT!

Knights & Castles

EXPLORING HISTORY THROUGH ART

ALEX MARTIN

Copyright © 2005 Two-Can Publishing and Toucan Books Ltd.

Two-Can Publishing
An imprint of Creative Publishing international, Inc.
18705 Lake Drive East
Chanhassen, MN 55317
1-800-328-3895
www.two-canpublishing.com

Created by
Toucan Books Ltd.
3rd Floor
89 Charterhouse Street
London EC1M 6HR

Project Manager: Ellen Dupont
Art Director: Bradbury and Williams
Editors: Miranda Baker, Kate Simkins
Designer: Bob Burroughs
Proofreader: Marion Dent
Indexer: Sue Bosanko
Picture Researcher: Christine Vincent
Series Consultant: David Wilkins

Library of Congress Cataloging-in-Publication Data

Martin, Alex.
Knights & castles : exploring history through art / Alex Martin.
p. cm. — (Picture that!)
Includes bibliographical references and index.
ISBN 1-58728-441-3 (hardcover with jacket)
1. Knights and knighthood—Juvenile literature. 2. Castles—Juvenile literature.
3. Civilization, Medieval—Juvenile literature. I. Title. II. Title: Knights and castles.
III. Series.
CR4513.M37 2005
940.1—dc22   20040114902

1 2 3 4 5 6 09 08 07 06 05 04

Printed in China

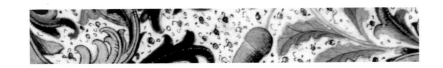

Contents

A Courtly Life

The age of knights and castles began more than 1,100 years ago in Europe. It was a period in history called the Middle Ages, which lasted until the 1500s.

PICTURE THIS: IT IS THE YEAR 1350. You are only seven years old, but you know that you want to become a knight. Because you are from a noble European family, your dream is a possibility. Soon you will leave your family's house and go to live with a knight as his page, or assistant. You will help him get dressed in the morning, take care of his clothes, and wait on him during meals. You will learn good manners and many other useful skills, such as dancing, singing, playing games, and writing poetry. Later, you hope to become your knight's squire. Then the knight will teach you how to handle weapons and horses, to lead men, and to manage an estate.

Finally, you will become a knight and begin a life of traveling and fighting.

Long ago, one Spanish knight described what his life was like: "Moldy bread and biscuit, meat cooked or raw; food today, none tomorrow. . . . Water from a pond or rain barrel, sleeping in the worst places, under a tent or branches, your armor still on your back and the enemy just an arrow's flight away."

But as a knight you will be well rewarded for these hard times. Winning a war means money, land, and honor for a knight. They may earn important titles such as lord or duke. The greatest of the knights build magnificent castles. A knight's home is large and clean, with tapestries on the walls, mats on the floors, and fires

THE FOUR STAGES of a knight's life are shown in this French painting: a child standing in a wheeled walking frame, a squire in fashionable clothes, a knight in armor, and a bent old man.

AT A JOUST, two knights demonstrated their skills in a mock battle, while courtiers and ladies enjoyed the show. Although the knights were not supposed to hurt each other, injuries were common.

to keep out the cold of winter.

You move to a knight's castle in the country. The castle grounds are like a small village, with workshops, stables, and gardens. In peaceful times, it is a place to relax and have fun. A knight and his guests enjoy hunting, jousting, or weapons practice by day, and feasts with storytelling and music by night.

But it is not uncommon for enemy armies to stage a surprise attack, or siege. The estate is prepared for such attacks. Soldiers live on the grounds, and there are supplies of food and weapons to help the estate survive a long battle.

The Middle Ages is a time when the trading of goods becomes a big business. Great churches, cities, and universities are built. Windmills for grinding wheat, rudders for steering ships, and the magnetic compass are invented.

Early in the Middle Ages, knights wore iron helmets and chain mail, a kind of armor made of interlaced metal rings. The men's castles stood on hilltops, surrounded by ditches and high wooden fences, or stockades. By the 1500s, armor develops into a suit of shining steel, and castles are built more for show than for protection.

When gunpowder is brought to Europe from China, the cannon replaces the longbow and sword. No armor will protect a knight against this powerful weapon of war.

LOVE AND FAME were the two goals of a knight's life. According to the code of chivalry, knights had to do daring deeds to win a lady's love. They were also expected to be generous and kind.

A Fortified City

KING CLOTHAR OF FRANCE LIES DYING IN A TENT JUST OUTSIDE THE CASTLE WALLS. His soldiers stand guard, waiting anxiously for news. Across the river, inside the walled estate, members of the king's family are already dividing up his kingdom.

The castle in the picture is the Île de la Cité, which stands in the center of Paris, France. The events shown in the picture took place in the year 561, but it was painted almost 900 years later. The style of the architecture, suits of armor, and weapons reflect what things looked like during the painter's own time, the 1450s.

The roofs, turrets, and chimneys along the skyline give an idea of just how many different buildings there were inside the castle walls. There would have been chapels, stables, government offices, halls for ceremonies and banquets, and living quarters for the royal family and all their servants.

Most castles were surrounded by an artificial moat, a water-filled ditch dug out by hand. The Île de la Cité (which means "City Island" in French) had a natural moat: the River Seine. This feature, along with its tall towers and high stone walls, made the city very difficult to attack.

Jean Fouquet (c. 1415–1481)

France's most famous fifteenth-century artist is Jean Fouquet, who worked in Rome and then in Paris as a royal painter. He was well known for his portraits, religious paintings, and a series of illuminated manuscripts—books illustrated with hand-painted pictures. Fouquet painted this picture for one of those books.

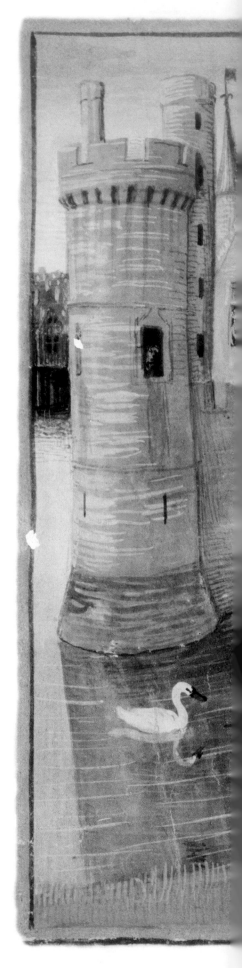

DEATH OF CLOTHAR I AND THE DIVISION OF HIS KINGDOM, 1459
JEAN FOUQUET

Symbol of France This French flag, adopted in 1357, shows three golden lilies, known as fleurs-de-lys *(flur-duh-LEE)*, on a bright blue background. According to legend, the Virgin Mary gave Clothar's father, King Clovis, a lily at his son's baptism. The lily is a symbol for purity.

Lookout A soldier defending the castle can peer through notches in the walls called battlements. He can easily duck right or left to avoid attackers' arrows. He will defend the castle by firing arrows or by throwing missiles or hot liquid.

Arrow slits People inside the castle can see through these narrow openings and shoot arrows out of them without being hit.

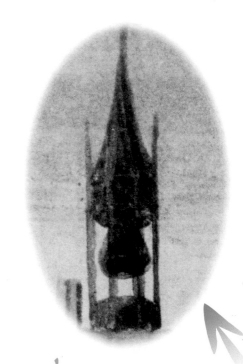

Telling the news Church bells are rung to send messages. A single bell is rung slowly to signal bad news, such as the death of a king or queen. That same bell may be rung quickly to sound an alarm. Bells are cast from bronze, then slowly shaved down until they ring at the right pitch.

Faithful birds The swan was a symbol of nobility, loyalty, and good faith. Although swans were greatly admired for their beauty, they were useful, too. Their meat was often served at banquets, and the soft feathers from the neck and breast were used to stuff pillows and quilts.

Triple trouble This weapon, called a halberd, has a blade for cutting and hacking, a point for thrusting, and a pick for stabbing through armor. It is a sword, spear, and ax, all in one weapon.

Dying king King Clothar is shown with a dagger in his neck, as if he had been murdered. It is true that Clothar was a violent man, but he actually died of a fever.

A Knight and His Lady

A YOUNG KNIGHT IS KNEELING IN FRONT OF THE LADY HE LOVES. He is in full armor, with his sword by his side. His gauntlets, helmet, and poleax lie on the ground beside him. The lady looks down at the knight. She is wearing a pointed headdress, known as a high henin, from which a lace veil hangs. Her red-and-gold velvet dress is trimmed with ermine fur, which only noble men and women wear. She has pale skin and a high forehead, both of which are very fashionable. (Medieval women often pluck hair from their foreheads to create this look.)

The scene painted on this decorative shield portrays the knight as a noble and romantic hero. Behind him stands a skeleton, a symbol for death. The skeleton is reaching out to grab the young warrior. *"Vous ou la mort,"* says the banner above them. This means "You or death" in French. The young knight loves this lady so desperately that he would die rather than be rejected by her.

This man's love for his lady is what inspires him to fulfill his knightly role. As a member of the knighthood, he is guided by rules called the code of chivalry. He must fight for the Christian faith, for the defenseless widow and the orphan child, and for justice, truth, and goodness.

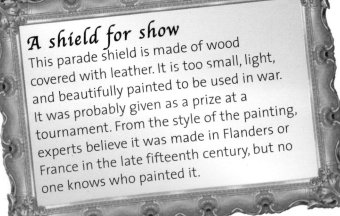

A shield for show
This parade shield is made of wood covered with leather. It is too small, light, and beautifully painted to be used in war. It was probably given as a prize at a tournament. From the style of the painting, experts believe it was made in Flanders or France in the late fifteenth century, but no one knows who painted it.

PAINTED PARADE SHIELD, FIFTEENTH CENTURY

Dark reminder
The skeleton reaching out for the knight is a symbol for death. The knight's life is a dangerous one, and he risks death every time he goes into battle.

Luxurious fabric
This dress is made from brocade, a patterned silk velvet from Italy that was popular with ladies in northern Europe. Flowers and leaves were common designs in the late 1400s, and the gold lace panel at the front of the dress was also very fashionable.

War helmet
The helmet is one of the most important parts of a suit of armor. It is made up of four pieces: the armet, or the main steel shell; the visor, a hinged piece covering the eyes and nose; the wrapper, or collar; and the crest, a design of feathers or painted symbols that identify the knight.

A Wedding Feast

IN A NOBLE HOUSEHOLD, A FEAST IS BEING HELD IN HONOR OF THE LADY CLARISSE, who is marrying a heroic French knight, Renaud de Montauban. On either side of the bride are waiting-damsels. The bridegroom and other male guests are sitting at a separate table.

Serving men wearing elegant pleated tunics and fashionable pointed shoes walk from table to table, followed by a hound hoping for some tasty scraps. On the left, one of the servers takes a pitcher of wine from the steward of the cellar, the servant in charge of the household's wine. On a balcony called the minstrels' gallery, three musicians entertain the couple and their guests. The tables are laid with fine linen cloths. The only other decoration is a rich canopy hanging over the bride's head.

As this painting shows, food and wine were served with great ceremony in wealthy households. There were strict rules about the order in which guests were served, the way meat and bread were cut, the pouring of the wine, and the prayers that were said before eating. A wedding feast such as this one would have consisted of many courses, mostly of meat and fish. The look of the dishes was considered as important as the taste.

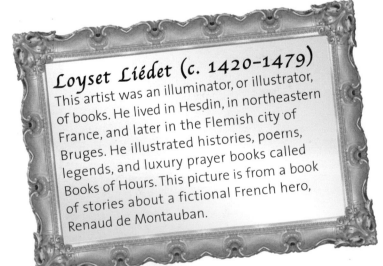

Loyset Liédet (c. 1420–1479)
This artist was an illuminator, or illustrator, of books. He lived in Hesdin, in northeastern France, and later in the Flemish city of Bruges. He illustrated histories, poems, legends, and luxury prayer books called Books of Hours. This picture is from a book of stories about a fictional French hero, Renaud de Montauban.

THE MARRIAGE FEAST, 1468
LOYSET LIÉDET

Wine for all Large amounts of wine or beer were drunk at banquets, but it was considered rude to drink too quickly or too much. Sometimes the wine was flavored with spices such as ginger and cinnamon. Water was not usually safe to drink, so people preferred wine.

School for style These well-dressed young men are carrying trays of food that may include roasted hedgehog, swan, or lark. The men are probably the sons of knights, working in a nobleman's household for a while in order to learn good manners, polite conversation, and the correct way of serving food and wine.

To the point These long, thin shoes made the wearer walk with tiny steps. Priests called such footwear vain and sinful.

*P*ass the salt The saler, or salt cellar, is a fancy container made of silver or gold, decorated with jewels and hung with charms to guard against poison. Its position on the table has a message for those seated there: guests sitting "above the salt" were of the highest rank, while those below were considered less important.

*T*he entertainers These musical instruments are called shawms. They are wooden tubes with finger holes and a double reed in the mouthpiece that vibrates to make a loud, rough sound. Shawms were brought to Europe from the Middle East.

*P*atterns on the floor These tiles have a fleur-de-lys (lily) design, which is the symbol of France. Tiles were shaped and decorated by hand, making them a luxury found only in wealthy homes. Most floors were made of packed soil, concrete, or wood.

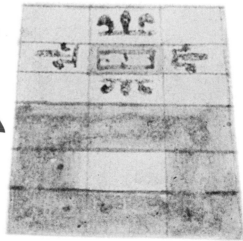

*T*he bride Clarisse has sections of ermine in her dress and a heart-shaped headdress decorated with gold and precious stones. Her hairstyle, with the top swept up into "horns," is very fashionable.

On the Estate

Society in the Middle Ages was divided into three main groups: knights, who protected people; priests, who prayed for people; and commoners, who grew food for everyone. Most commoners lived and worked on a knight's estate.

PICTURE THIS: YOU LIVE IN A CASTLE. IT IS THE HOME AND WORKPLACE FOR DOZENS, OR PERHAPS EVEN HUNDREDS, OF PEOPLE. The lord, or owner of the estate, and his lady are attended by other knights and ladies-in-waiting, each of whom has their own gentlemen and gentlewomen to serve them. There are clerks to run the kitchens and cellars, bailiffs to manage the estate, grooms for the horses, huntsmen, carpenters, cooks, laundrywomen, gardeners, and household servants. There may also be a priest for the chapel, and singers and musicians for entertainment. You are a page to one of the knights, hoping to be a knight yourself when you grow up.

The lord and lady live in the grandest possible style. They spend time with their many guests and attendants, hunting, jousting, eating, drinking, singing, and dancing. Dinner is a fancy affair, held at night in the hall of the castle. The lord and lady and their guests enjoy gigantic amounts of food, wine, and beer. You help serve it. The next morning, the leftovers are handed out to the poor.

The farms, villages, and forests around the castle are all part of the lord's estate. People called peasants work the land and give the lord their best produce as rent. They do all the hard work, such as constructing new buildings, making repairs, and building roads and fences.

It is important for farmers to do their job properly, sowing and harvesting their crops at the right time, taking good care of their animals, and storing their produce in the right way. If a crop fails or spoils too quickly after the

SPINNING AND WEAVING were done by the women of the house. At the bottom of this picture, a lady separates the wool into strands so that it can be spun into yarn by the woman behind her (top right). The lady on the left uses a loom to weave the yarn into cloth.

GRAPES WERE STOMPED with bare feet to press out the juice.

WHEAT WAS HARVESTED with a sickle, then made into flour.

WORKERS collected the harvested grapes in baskets.

PIGS ATE ACORNS that were knocked down from oak trees.

harvest, the farmers and their families will starve. The weather plays an important part, too. Not enough rain, or too much, can be a disaster.

For rich and poor alike, life is short. Even in good times, most people live no longer than thirty years. Half of all children die before they are seven years old, weakened by diseases that are spread through dirty living conditions.

Because life is so risky, people pray to God for help and protection. They also give one-tenth of their produce, known as a tithe, to the church. They believe that this will please God and keep them safe in this life and the next.

Country roads are dusty in summer and muddy and wet in winter, so travel is slow. Many country people spend their lives in one place, never moving more than a few miles from the house where they were born. However, because you are going to be a knight when you grow up, you know that you will travel the world.

You feel lucky to be a page, even though you have to work hard and live far from your family. You are one of the few children who will learn to read and write. Most children begin farm work as soon they are strong enough, learning from their parents how to work the land, keep animals, and cook and preserve food.

HUNTING WITH FALCONS was a favorite sport of the rich. These birds, specially trained by falconers to hunt rabbits and small birds, were carried on a thick gauntlet, or glove, and kept hooded until the moment the hunter released them.

Hunting Deer

HUNTING WAS A FAVORITE SPORT OF KINGS, LORDS, AND KNIGHTS, and a popular way of entertaining noble guests. One medieval French nobleman, Gaston de Foix, wrote a book about why he loved to hunt. In the book, he says that hunting is dangerous and exciting, a display of skill and strength. He writes about the thrilling sounds: the blowing of the hunting horns, the baying of the dogs, and the shouts of the huntsmen. And he talks about the splendid feasts that come at the end of each day's hunt.

Wealthy noblemen kept whole estates just for hunting and spent huge amounts of money on dogs, hawks, kennelmen, and huntsmen, as well as expensive collars, leashes, horns, and weapons. They built their castles near forests that could provide them with good hunting.

Stag hunting was considered a particularly noble sport. Hunters were careful to hunt only fully grown male deer, and many men felt sympathy for a beast as it faced its death. It reminded them that their own lives must end, no matter how wealthy and important they were.

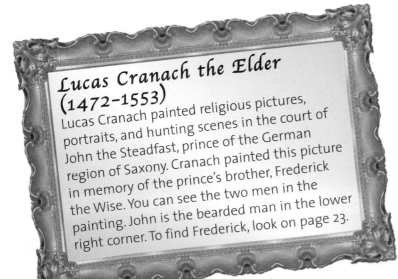

Lucas Cranach the Elder (1472–1553)

Lucas Cranach painted religious pictures, portraits, and hunting scenes in the court of John the Steadfast, prince of the German region of Saxony. Cranach painted this picture in memory of the prince's brother, Frederick the Wise. You can see the two men in the painting. John is the bearded man in the lower right corner. To find Frederick, look on page 23.

THE STAG HUNT, 1529 LUCAS CRANACH THE ELDER

On the leash These greyhounds are fast, agile dogs that are specially trained to chase deer. The dogs are led on leashes to different parts of the forest and released when a deer runs past. After the hunt, they will be rewarded with scraps of meat and pieces of bread soaked in the deer's blood.

Noble guest This man with the magnificent fur hat must be a very important guest, because he has been chosen to kill the wounded deer with his sword. This honor is granted by the lord who organized the hunt.

A spectator sport Sometimes the ladies of an estate joined the hunt, but often they chose to watch from a safe distance. These ladies are out of range of the hunters' crossbows, but they are in a good position to see the most dramatic moment of the hunt. The men in the boat carry spears to protect them from wild animals.

Music of the hunt Huntsmen blew their horns for two reasons: to add to the noise and excitement, and to communicate with other hunters. A special code of long and short blasts allowed them to send messages such as, "Get ready!", "I've seen a stag!" or "Call up your hounds!" Later, the mouthpiece of the horn was plugged with grass and the instrument was filled with wine to toast the day's hunt.

Hide and seek In the type of hunting shown in this painting, dogs chased the deer out of the forest into an open space. The hunters hid behind trees, waiting to fire at the deer with crossbows. This gentleman is Frederick the Wise. His servant has a tool to wind up the crossbow so it will be ready to fire again. Even if the servant works fast, the crossbow can be fired only twice in 60 seconds.

Life on the Land

IT IS AUTUMN IN THE COUNTRYSIDE, AND THE GRAIN HAS BEEN HARVESTED AND BROUGHT INTO THE CASTLE. Now it is time to sow the seeds for next year. The sower (in lower right corner of the painting) has filled his apron from the sack at the edge of the field and is scattering handfuls of seeds over the freshly plowed earth. Nearby, another farmer rides one of a team of two horses that are dragging a harrow behind them. This heavy frame covers the newly scattered seeds with a thin layer of soil.

While it was common for men to do heavy work such as plowing and sowing, women worked on the farm as well. They weeded the fields and helped tend the animals. The whole family worked together to bring in the harvest.

Not everyone who lived in the country worked on farms. Some made their living from local rivers by catching and selling fish, washing clothes, or transporting goods from place to place by boat. These were hard jobs. There were no engines to drive the boats and no machines to clean the clothes.

Only a few people knew how to read, write, and work with numbers. These people, like the elegantly dressed customs officers sitting in front of the castle gate, did not have to do such physical work.

Gerard Horenbout (1465-1541)

This picture comes from a prayer book owned by Domenico Grimani, a cardinal (Catholic high priest) who lived in Venice, Italy. It was painted in about 1515 by Gerard Horenbout, who came from Flanders. An illuminated prayer book like this, written and painted by hand, took about two years to make.

Standing guard This man is trying to keep some hungry crows from eating the freshly scattered seeds. This job was often done by children, who would use stones, rattles, or clappers to scare off the birds.

GRIMANI BREVIARY, c. 1515
GERARD HORENBOUT

Telling time Public clocks like this one, high on a tower, allowed ordinary people to tell time accurately. Clocks were a recent invention: the first public chiming clock was built in Milan, Italy, in 1335. Before this, people measured time by the movement of the sun.

New technology The collar these horses are wearing was also a new invention. Made of wood and padded leather, the collar helped spread the weight of the harrow across the horses' chest and shoulders.

Laundry Clothes and bedsheets were usually washed in a stream or river. Soap was a luxury, so women usually rubbed the cloth against stones to remove the dirt. This was hard on the fabric and made it wear out quickly, so people did not wash their clothes very often.

Tax man The two customs officers sit at a table outside the castle gates, collecting taxes from anyone who is bringing goods to sell in the town. The money they collect will go to the king, who may use it to pay for wars or for public projects such as roads and ports.

A good shove It was easier and cheaper to transport goods by water than by land. This barge, weighed down with goods, needs a crew of six strong men. They push their poles against the river bed to drive the boat upstream. They float with the current downstream.

Horse power In northern Europe, the rich, heavy soil made working the land slow and difficult. Plowing and harrowing became much easier once people found ways to use horses to do the work.

Inside a Farmhouse

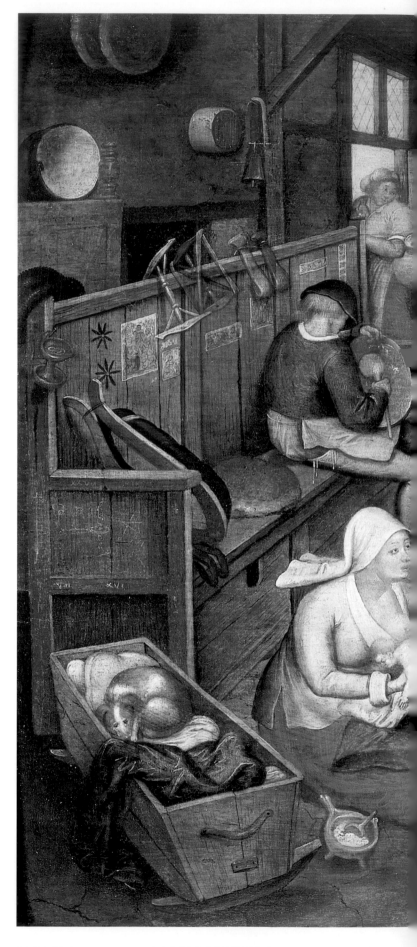

NOT EVERYONE IN THE COUNTRYSIDE LIVED LIKE LORDS AND KNIGHTS. Peasants had to pay rent to the lord of the estate for living on his land. Payment was made in food or in fuel such as peat or wood.

Peasants worked hard to have enough left over to support their families. It was a hard life, as this picture shows. The farmer and his wife look very tired. Their cottage is smoky and dark. It is packed with tools, baskets, food, pets, furniture, and people. Everything happens in this room. It is a kitchen, dairy, storeroom, workshop, living room, and playroom all in one. There is no place to go to get away from all the activity.

Even so, this family is better off than some peasants. Their home is fairly large, and there are plenty of hands to help with the chores. The stew cooking over the fire and the bread on the table show that they are well fed.

In this scene, some wealthy visitors, perhaps from the castle, have arrived. The farmer, to the right of the cooking pot, is humbly accepting a gift from the gentleman in the cloak. The visitors, standing stiffly in their fine clothes, look uncomfortable.

Pieter Bruegel the Younger (1564–1638)

Pieter Bruegel was the son of one of the most famous artists of his time. He earned a good living by making copies of his father's most popular works, including *Children's Games* on page 50. Pieter was a very skilled painter himself. He specialized in painting detailed scenes of country life like this one.

VISIT TO THE FARM, 1598 PIETER BRUEGEL THE YOUNGER

*D*airy products These two peasants are using a butter churn. As they push the pole up and down, paddles turn inside the churn, whipping the cream inside into butter. The family will use some of the butter for cooking and eating. The rest will be sold.

*M*an's best friend Dogs were useful for herding livestock, hunting, and guarding the farm. But they were also kept as pets. In this picture, one of the two dogs is sleeping in the baby's cradle. These animals are very much a part of the family.

*F*resh water This girl is on her way out to the well. She will haul up the water in a bucket. Then she will pour the water into the pitcher she is carrying. She will use this pitcher to bring the water into the house and to store it until it is needed for cooking or washing.

*F*arm tools These scissors are used for clipping the fleece from sheep. The fleece is washed, combed, and spun into wool thread. The thread is then woven into cloth for making warm winter clothes.

*T*he visitor This lady is probably taking money from her purse to give to the child. The church encouraged rich people to give money to the poor and needy, saying that these good deeds would be rewarded in heaven.

At War

Knights were trained warriors, and the many wars and battles fought in medieval Europe meant that they used their fighting skills often.

PICTURE THIS: IT IS 1356. YOU ARE THIRTEEN YEARS OLD AND SERVE A KNIGHT AS HIS SQUIRE. You carry his helmet and banner and help him put on his heavy armor. In return, he teaches you about fighting and the art of war so that you, too, can become a knight some day. You learn to use a lance and a sword and you become an expert horseman. You also study arithmetic, grammar, astronomy, and music.

Knights have been given land and titles by the king in return for their help in times of war. A knight devotes himself to a noble cause, such as defending his king.

When knights go to war, they fight alongside archers and foot soldiers. The army also includes people who take care of the baggage, transportation, tents, weapons, and horses.

Wars give the archers and foot soldiers the chance to become wealthy, too, but not in the noble way a knight earns his living. When an army captures a town or a village, soldiers loot houses and shops. They take jewels, coins, clothes, furniture, tools, animals—whatever they can find. Prisoners can also be valuable. The richer and more important a prisoner is, the more money the kidnappers get for freeing him.

As a squire during the fourteenth century, you see the latest weapons, including the longbow

THIS SUIT OF ARMOR is beautifully decorated. It belonged to a German prince, Christian I of Saxony.

GIRDING WITH A SWORD was an important moment in the knighting ceremony. The man on the left is buckling the belt that holds the new knight's sword.

and the cannon. Knights wear suits of armor made by skilled craftsmen. To test the armor's strength, the craftsmen fire crossbows at it. You are amazed to see that the weapons barely make a dent in the steel armor. These crossbows easily would have killed an unprotected man.

Still, warfare has not changed much in hundreds of years. Battles usually begin with a charge by knights on horseback. The defenders shoot at them with crossbows or longbows, hoping to turn them back with a deadly rain of arrows. They may also send out a wave of mounted knights to meet the attack. Then the two armies come together, and hand-to-hand fighting begins. Fallen horses and men, broken weapons, and armor soon litter the battlefield.

The battle is over when one side gives up or turns back. Then the armies care for the wounded and bury the dead near the battle site. Officials called heralds from both armies agree on a name for the battle. It is usually named after the nearest village.

LIKE THEIR RIDERS, HORSES ARE protected by heavy armor when they go to war. The designs and colors worn by the knight and his horse allow their army to recognize them from afar. The horses are specially trained not to panic or shy away in a charge. Many horses are killed or injured in the fighting.

On the Battlefield

IT IS A SUMMER DAY, AND A BATTLE IS RAGING. As trumpets blare, lances smash into armor and knights fall from their horses. Men and animals lie dying on the ground. In a flurry of hand-to-hand fighting, daggers and swords flash and axes and maces fly. The air is filled with the sounds of men shouting, horses neighing, wood splintering, and steel clashing against steel.

On a hillside in the distance, men load and shoot crossbows. Foot soldiers with spears and axes appear from behind a hill to chase the weakened enemy.

The Battle of San Romano was fought in Italy on June 1, 1432, between the armies of the city of Florence (shown on the left) and the cities of Lucca, Siena, and Milan (on the right). Florence won. Around fifteen thousand men were involved in the day-long battle. The painting shows the different stages of the battle as if they are all happening at once.

In the distance, a hound chases three hares across a field. The hound may stand for Florence, and the hares may be the three defeated enemies. The hares, like many of the soldiers on the right side of the picture, are doing the sensible thing—running away.

THE BATTLE OF SAN ROMANO, 1456 PAOLO UCCELLO

Paolo Uccello (1397–1475)

This artist's real name was Paolo di Dono, but he is always referred to as Uccello. He may have gotten this name from his love of birds. (*Uccello* is the Italian word for *bird*.) He lived in Florence, Italy. He is famous for his interest in perspective (using size and color to give depth to an image) and his crowded, colorful paintings.

W̲ell-protected A full suit of fifteenth-century armor is made up of 27 separate pieces of curved steel, joined with metal rivets and leather straps. It is very heavy, weighing 50 pounds (25 kg) or more. Underneath, the knight wears a chain-mail shirt and padded clothing. A colorful scarf or a crest of feathers identifies the knight who is hidden behind the steel mask.

T̲ake aim The crossbow is the most accurate weapon for long-distance attacks. It fires a short, iron-tipped arrow, known as a bolt, up to 1,300 feet (400 m). The weapon's power comes from a tightly stretched string, which is pulled back by turning a handle. This process makes the weapon very slow to load.

Heavy metal The mace, or war hammer, can be used for knocking a man down or stunning him with a blow to the helmet. Its sharp tip can pierce armor. But the knight using this mace is open to attack. With his arm raised, there is a gap in his armor where he could be wounded by a sword or a spear.

Hand-to-hand fighting A knight in full armor moves very slowly on foot. Here, one knight has knocked off another man's helmet and has him at his mercy. If he takes the man prisoner, he can exchange him later, either for ransom money or for a fellow knight taken prisoner by the enemy.

Charging horses Bulging eyes and flared nostrils are signs of a horse terrified by the violence of war. Although horses usually wore armor in battle, Uccello painted these horses without it. No one knows why. Perhaps he wanted to show their beauty and grace. He was well known for his love of animals.

A Legendary Hero

SAINT GEORGE WAS THE PATRON SAINT OF SOLDIERS, AND THE PERFECT HERO. St. George's story is told in *The Golden Legend*, a popular book of saints' lives written in the thirteenth century. In the legend of St. George, he rescues a girl from a ferocious dragon. In fact, he rescues a whole city, because the dragon was eating all the cattle, sheep, and humans it could find. People are so amazed by George's bravery that they decide to become Christians like him.

No one knows whether St. George was a real person or not. Some believe that he was a soldier who was killed by the Romans in the third century. Many people had faith in his saintly power, especially during the Crusades. This was a series of wars in which European Christians fought Muslims for the control of the Holy Land. Soldiers in several battles said they had seen St. George fighting on their side.

In 1348, St. George became the patron saint of England. His banner—a red cross on a white background, shown on his chest in this picture—was adopted as the English flag. (You can also see St. George's flag on the trumpets in the painting *The Battle of San Romano*, on page 34.) Carrying a saint's banner was a way of asking for that saint's protection.

Every knight had to dedicate himself to a lady, and St. George was no exception. The calm, beautiful girl in the painting shows no fear, in spite of the horrible scene in front of her. She knows that St. George is going to win. Just about everything in this picture, from the shining saint and his magnificent horse to the ships anchored in the bay, gives the happy impression that things will turn out well in the end.

Watching the show The people standing on the balconies are looking up at the hill where St. George is fighting the dragon. Perhaps they are waiting for a sign that the dragon is dead.

Pedro Nisart

Pedro Nisart is like St. George—no one really knows who he was. There are two known pictures by this brilliant artist, both painted in about 1470 in Palma, the city shown in this picture, which is on the island of Majorca. The only clue about him is his name. Pedro Nisart may have come from Nice, a town in France.

ST. GEORGE AND THE DRAGON, c. 1470
PEDRO NISART

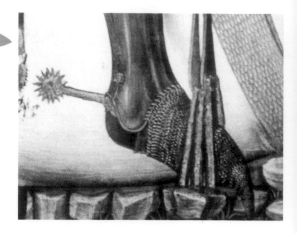

Fancy footwork

Only a knight was allowed to wear spurs. He strapped them to his feet and pressed them into his horse's sides to make it go faster. These elegant golden spurs were the height of fashion in the fifteenth century.

Death's head

The skull under the horse is a reminder that before St. George's arrival, the dragon killed many people.

Guiding hand

A knight held the horse's reins in his left hand, keeping his right hand free for a lance or sword. In earlier days, before steel armor was developed, he would also have carried a shield on his left arm. St. George's reins, like his clothing and armor, are beautifully decorated.

Tower of strength A drawbridge is lowered, and the town's defenders rush out. The battlements at the top of the tower and along the city walls jut out to make the walls harder to climb. The holes underneath allow soldiers to drop stones, burning tar, boiling water, or hot sand onto the heads of attackers.

Good works Two generous citizens hand over their saddlebags (probably full of money) to a monk in front of his chapel. Everyone had to give one-tenth of their earnings to the church. People believed this would help them stay safe in this life and go to heaven when they died.

Wind power Far in the distance stands a windmill, grinding wheat to make flour. In the painting, this is a symbol of peace and prosperity. Windmills came into use in Europe in the late twelfth century.

A Successful Invasion

In September 1066, a huge army invaded England. The story of this invasion is told in pictures and words in the Bayeux Tapestry. Harold of England had promised the English crown to William, the Duke of Normandy, but then he made himself king instead. When William heard the news, he was so angry that he decided to take England by force. He built a huge fleet and sailed across the English Channel with 7,000 men, as well as horses, armor, weapons, food, wine, tents, and other equipment.

At the Battle of Hastings, the attacking French army defeated the English defenders. King Harold was killed when an arrow hit him in the eye, and William became king of England. For a time, French (the language of the Normans) replaced Anglo-Saxon as the official language. Life in England changed forever.

The scene shown here is only a small part of the Bayeux Tapestry. In this section, Harold has just been crowned king. Suddenly, a comet appears. People wonder if it means bad luck for the new king of England.

THE BAYEUX TAPESTRY, 1073–1083, ARTISTS UNKNOWN

The Bayeux Tapestry

The tapestry is made of colored threads embroidered on a strip of linen measuring 23 feet (7 m) long by 20 inches (50 cm) wide. It was probably made in the English city of Canterbury. The tapestry, now almost 1,000 years old, is on display in the town of Bayeux, France. Because it is made up of a series of images that tell a story, it is often described as an early comic strip.

Sky light This is Halley's Comet, which can be seen from Earth every 75 years. It was first recorded in China in 240 B.C. and last appeared in 1984. In 1066, the comet appeared in the sky on every clear night from February to May. People did not know what it was and were frightened when they saw it.

Message in the heavens People believed that planets and stars could affect their health and fortune and that unusual events in the sky, such as comets or eclipses of the moon, were warnings from God.

Sailing to France These men are messengers from England who are sailing to France to tell William that Harold is now king. They sail in a typical warship of the time: long and low, with a single mast, a square sail, and a carved dragon at each end. These ships, based on Viking longships, also had oars, although only one of them—the steering oar—is shown here. These boats are open, so there is no shelter in a storm.

Bad news This messenger is telling Harold that the comet has appeared. Harold listens carefully. Feeling guilty about his broken promise to William, he will have bad dreams about a ghostly fleet of ships.

A Town under Siege

LAYING SIEGE TO A TOWN IS ONE OF THE OLDEST MILITARY STRATEGIES. In medieval times, towns were protected by high walls and heavy gates, but an enemy army could surround it and keep food and water from coming in. Eventually hunger or thirst would force the people to surrender. But attackers could not keep a town under siege forever—their army would go home if they were not paid their wages or when winter came.

The rules for a siege were simple. The leader of the attacking army came to the gates and called for the town to surrender. If they agreed, the people inside were allowed to leave in peace with their possessions. If they refused and the town was captured, their town might be robbed and destroyed, and they might all be killed.

In the Middle Ages, powerful siege weapons, such as catapults, rams, cannons, and mortars, were developed. Attackers built high, rolling platforms called siege towers from which they could fight. But townspeople made preparations, too. They built sturdier walls and dug traps outside the walls that would make siege towers fall over.

In this picture, the siege of the French town of Ribodane is coming to an end. The walls are being destroyed with pickaxes, the main gate is open, and English soldiers are marching in.

Chronique d'Angleterre

This picture is an illustration from the *Chronique d'Angleterre*, which is French for "Chronicles of England." The book was written by Jean de Wavrin, Lord of Forestal, a knight and historian who lived from about 1415 to 1475. The beautifully illustrated book was made in Belgium in the late 1400s. No one knows the name of the artist.

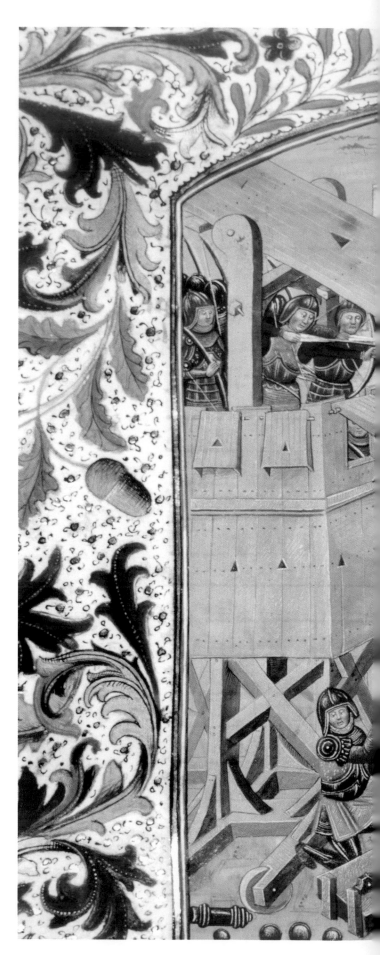

TAKING OF RIBODANE, LATE FIFTEENTH CENTURY

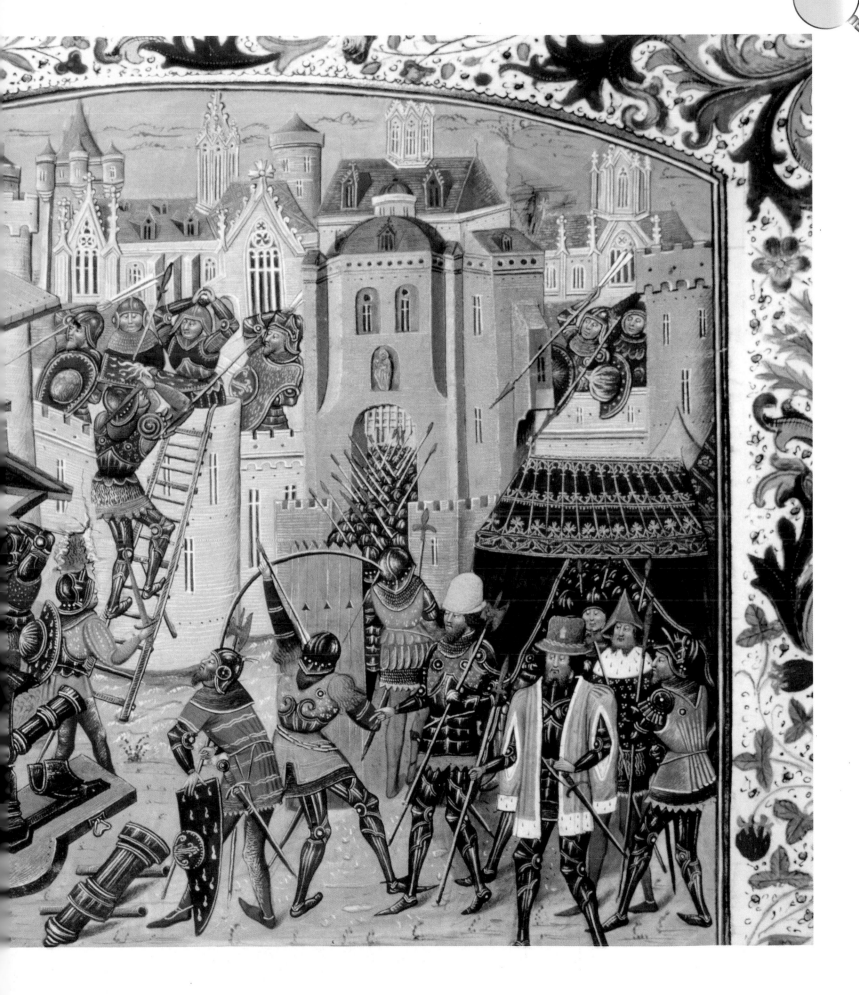

Portcullis The gatehouse is protected by a heavy gate made of wood covered with iron, which can be raised and lowered as needed. Another device for keeping out attackers was an L-shaped entrance passage. Defenders could wait around the corner to surprise the enemy.

Taking aim The gunner using this cannon can adjust the angle and height of his shot by sliding a bolt into one of the holes in the curved bar at the back off the cannon.

A risky position

Siege ladders can be hooked over the tops of castle walls. Climbing a ladder was the most dangerous method of attack, because the soldiers defending the town could throw things down at the men climbing up. This man is about to have a cannonball dropped on his head!

Smash and grab

A break in the city's wall means the beginning of the end for Ribodane. Attackers can now rush in and kill the people inside.

Rapid fire

A good archer could fire twelve arrows a minute, to a distance of over 700 feet (210 m). The longbow he used was made of wood and was over 6 feet (2 m) long. Skillful use of the longbow gave English armies a great advantage over their enemies during the 1300s, but by the time of this battle, both sides had even more deadly weapons, such as the cannon.

Instant cover

The heavy wooden shutters on this siege tower can be swung open for attack or closed for protection, all in a matter of seconds. Triangular peepholes let the archers inside the tower choose their moment to lift the shutter and shoot their arrows.

Festivals and Fun

Life in the Middle Ages was difficult, but there was always time for fun. Children made up their own games, and everyone enjoyed fairs, tournaments, traveling theaters, and holidays.

PICTURE THIS: YOU ARE A SQUIRE. THE KNIGHT WITH WHOM YOU TRAIN HAS EARNED THE TITLE OF DUKE. Soon he will marry a foreign princess, and he wants to impress her.

For nine days, the duke holds jousts and feasts in his lady's honor. His clothes and even his horse are decorated with jewels. The tables are set with the best linens and dishes. You help serve the food and wine. Acrobats, jugglers, singers, and jesters entertain everyone. You have never seen such riches or had so much fun.

Good times such as these are rare in the Middle Ages. A disease called the Black Death kills one in every three people in the mid-1300s. Some wars go on for years. Without medicine, electricity, drains, or running water, life is hard. Even so, people still find ways to enjoy themselves. But the rich and poor lead very different lives.

Knights can enjoy themselves all they want when they are not at war. They hunt, feast, and attend jousts and tournaments. They may visit the palace of the king or the castles of noble friends. Kings and nobles show off their wealth by spending fortunes on weapons, horses, dogs, and fine clothing.

Ladies bring glamour and romance to the court. They are admired not only for their beauty but also for their singing and dancing, witty conversation, intelligence, and goodness.

As a squire or knight during the Middle Ages, you learn a number of popular games: chess,

THE FIRST CAROLS were dances that were performed at all joyful times of year, not just at Christmas. Although dancing was often condemned by the Church, it was a popular form of entertainment and exercise.

COURT JESTERS were professional clowns who helped their masters forget their cares. They told jokes and silly stories, sang funny songs, and performed magic tricks. Jesters wore brightly colored costumes and hats with bells to add to the fun.

checkers, and card games have been brought to Europe from India and Persia by knights returning from the Crusades or by Muslims from southern Spain.

Cards and board games are too expensive for all but the richest families to own. Peasant children make up their own games. Peasants can also attend fairs, tournaments, and traveling theater productions.

DANCING WAS AS POPULAR with working people as with the nobility. In 1374, a dancing mania spread across Germany, Holland, and Flanders. People danced until they were exhausted and had visions of saints and angels.

Churches are an important part of peoples' religious and social lives. Each church has a patron saint, with a special day set aside in his or her honor. On the saint's day, and on the Christian holidays of Easter, Whitsun, Corpus Christi, and Christmas, local churches hold festivals with processions and plays performed in the streets. Non-Christian holidays, such as Midsummer's Day and the Feast of Fools, are also causes for celebrating. In many parts of Europe, carnival is a wild time of drinking, eating, and fun that leads up to Lent, a period of fasting and prayer before Easter.

Children's Games

TWO HUNDRED CHILDREN PLAYING EIGHTY-FOUR DIFFERENT GAMES! In this picture, Pieter Bruegel turns a busy town into a giant playground. It is an amazing and unusual record of the period in which he lived. Anyone could look out of the window and see children playing in the streets, fields, or farmyards, but artists rarely recorded such scenes.

The medieval children are doing some of the same things that children today do for fun. They climb on walls, trees, and fences. They swim in ponds and streams. They pretend to be brides, parents, and shopkeepers. They hold their own parades, races, jousts, and contests. You can see all these games, and many others, in the painting.

Toys were made out of whatever a child could find: sticks, stones, bits of rope or leather, barrels, bones, or bricks. More fancy toys such as hobbyhorses, hoops for rolling down the street, or tops (look for these under the arches of the building in the center), would probably have been made by a parent or bought at a traveling fair.

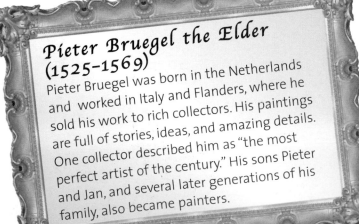

Pieter Bruegel the Elder (1525–1569)

Pieter Bruegel was born in the Netherlands and worked in Italy and Flanders, where he sold his work to rich collectors. His paintings are full of stories, ideas, and amazing details. One collector described him as "the most perfect artist of the century." His sons Pieter and Jan, and several later generations of his family, also became painters.

CHILDREN'S GAMES, 1560 PIETER BRUEGEL THE ELDER

Playtime
Until age six or seven, children were allowed to play all day. After that, poor children had to work. Wealthy children began their education. Boys became pages or studied to be priests. Girls learned needlework, dancing, and other skills of proper ladies.

Learning to swim
These children have blown up a pig's bladder to help them float in the water.

Making toys
Children have always enjoyed making things with their hands. The boy on the left has built a toy mill. The one on the right is using willow twigs to make pointed hats and a cage for a pet bird. The boy in the middle is blowing bubbles with a pipe.

*B*oys' clothes Some of these boys look as if they are wearing dresses. They are actually wearing long coats or knee-length tunics called shifts. They wear narrow pants underneath. Girls wear long dresses.

*T*ug-of-war Here, two boys on each side are pretending to be a horse, while a third boy, the knight, sits on each horse's back. The two knights try to pull each other across a line marked on the ground.

*R*olling along The hoop is a popular toy. It is pushed along with a stick, which can be tricky but fun. The exercise will also help a child stay warm in winter. This hoop has bells around the inside that jingle as it rolls.

*P*aint shop This girl is grinding a brick and weighing out the dust to sell in her shop. Artists used this colored dust as a pigment, or coloring, for their paints. Bruegel would have used it to paint the buildings—and the brick—in this picture!

The Goldsmith's Shop

A YOUNG COUPLE, PERHAPS MEMBERS OF THE DUKE OF BURGUNDY'S COURT, is visiting a goldsmith to buy an engagement ring. It is an important moment: a wedding not only means that a man and a woman are pledging their love to one another, but also that two families are joining fortunes.

Jewelry was often worn to show a person's rank. Rare and expensive materials were also believed to bring health, wealth, and good luck.

Goldsmiths were important people. They worked with precious metals and stones, and the things they made were used in church, at home, and on special occasions.

Some examples of their work can be seen in this shop. On the top shelf are wine jugs decorated with gold bands. The mayor of the city might give jugs like these as presents to important visitors. Below them hangs a buckle, the perfect size for the bride's sash on the counter. The jar with the golden lid will be used in church. There are also rings, brooches, pendants, and the goldsmith's precious raw materials—amber, pearls, emeralds, and rubies. Behind them are pieces of coral, porphyry, and crystal, which were thought to have magical powers.

Petrus Christus (c. 1415–1473)

Petrus Christus lived in Bruges, a wealthy city in Flanders that was known for its canals and fine houses. Little is known about him, not even the exact dates of his birth and death, but several of his bright, beautifully painted works have survived to this day. This painting shows the patron saint of goldsmiths, St. Eligius, at work like any ordinary person.

Good-luck charms The items displayed here all have a special purpose. Coral protects against envy, lightning, poison, black magic, war, and death at sea. Rubies bring joy, prosperity, and peace. Emeralds and sapphires improves one's eyesight and memory. People believe pearls are the dews of heaven, and that they bring good health. Crystal is meant to save people from nightmares.

A GOLDSMITH IN HIS SHOP, 1449
PETRUS CHRISTUS

Poison detectors
People believed these fossilized shark's teeth, known as serpents' tongues, would change color or start sweating if they came into contact with poison. Many people lived in fear of being poisoned by their enemies and were prepared to pay a high price for items that would protect them.

In the balance
The goldsmith weighs the ring on his scales. This image would remind Christians that at the Last Judgment, God would weigh their good deeds against their sins.

Magic cup This drinking goblet is made from a coconut shell. Coconuts were thought to be good for the health and to act against the effects of poison. Rulers often had servants taste their food first to be sure their enemies had not poisoned it.

Message in gold This beautifully decorated gold jar has a pelican on top. Legends say that pelicans peck their own breasts to feed their young with blood. The wine served during Holy Communion in a Christian church represents the blood of Christ, and the pelican is often used as a symbol of the Christian religion.

Honesty guaranteed The mirror shows two people looking in from the street outside. By law, goldsmiths had to work in public, so everyone could see that they were using only the best materials. The man holding the falcon is wealthy and fashionable, a typical customer for such a jeweler.

The Joust

The year is 1390. At St. Inglevert, on the north coast of France, French and English knights meet for a grand tournament. Against a colorful background of canvas "castles" and boldly patterned shields and banners, ladies and courtiers watch the knights gallop toward each other on horseback. Knights hold their lances tight under their right arms and their shields on the left. They brace themselves for the jolt that will send one of them clattering to the ground.

Tournaments were held at royal weddings and birthdays, and on special political occasions.

They began as a way for knights to test their skills, but soon they became a popular form of entertainment and a favorite sport of the rich and noble.

In one contest called the mêlée, two teams of knights fought each other. In the quintain, a single knight charged at a target. A joust was a battle between two single knights on horseback. In these contests, knights did not usually want to injure their opponents. They just wanted to prove their courage to the ladies and to win fame and fortune. The tournament ended with prizes, feasting, singing and dancing.

TOURNAMENT OF ST. INGLEVERT, FIFTEENTH CENTURY ARTIST UNKNOWN

All for love Before the joust, the heralds who organize the event will ask the ladies to give a symbol of their admiration to the bravest and best of the knights. Each knight wears a scarf or sleeve given to him by his favorite lady.

A medieval historian
Jean Froissart (c. 1337–1410) wrote a chronicle, or history, of the 1300s. His book is full of details about how people lived in those days. A beautifully illustrated copy of this book, called an illuminated manuscript, is in the British Library in London, and this picture comes from that manuscript. No one knows who painted it.

War games Each knight holds a brightly colored shield, decorated with his coat of arms. He uses this to protect himself from his opponent's lance. The knights are accompanied by their squires.

Protecting the horses Horses are draped with padded cloths called caparisons to protect them from injury. The wooden barrier keeps the horses from crashing into each other as they charge.

Glossary

Anglo-Saxon people from Germany (the Angles, Saxons, and Jutes) who settled in Britain starting in the fifth century A.D. The term also describes their language.

archer a person who is skilled with a bow and arrow

architecture the style and design of buildings

armor a suit of metal worn by knights to protect them during battle

banquet a fancy meal

barge a large, flat wooden boat for carrying heavy loads

Black Death a deadly disease, also called bubonic plague, that is spread by rats and fleas

cannon a large gun that fires large iron or stone balls

castle a large, strong building or group of buildings surrounded by a high wall for protection

chain mail small iron rings linked to form a protective layer of clothing for a soldier

comet an enormous ball of ice and dust that travels through space and leaves behind a trail of glittering vapor

courtier a family member, friend, or advisor to a king or queen

Crusades a series of wars in which Christian armies tried to capture the Holy Land (Palestine) from its Muslim rulers

dagger a pointed knife

estate the land belonging to a castle. Also one of three social classes: nobility, priests, and peasants

falcon a bird of prey used by hunters to help them hunt smaller animals

gauntlet a knight's glove

harrow a wooden frame with iron blades that is dragged over a plowed field to break the soil into smaller pieces or to cover new seeds with soil

herald an official who makes public announcements and arranges ceremonies

Timeline

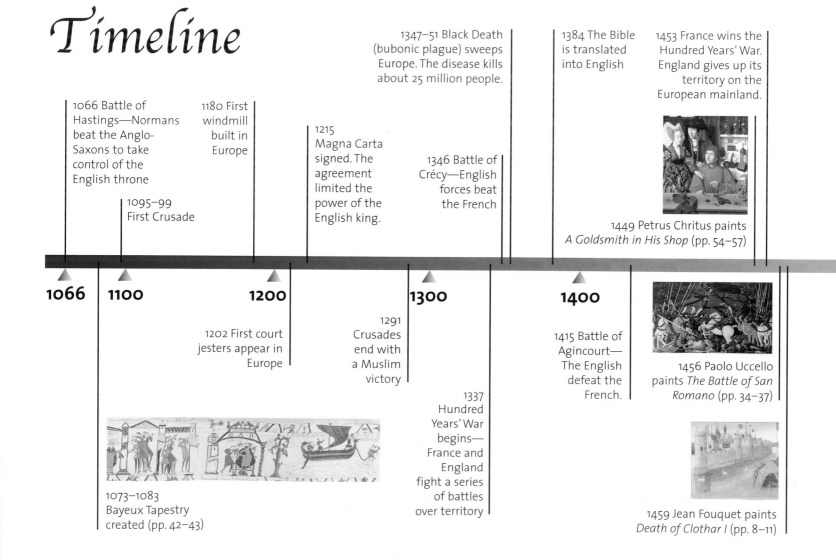

1347–51 Black Death (bubonic plague) sweeps Europe. The disease kills about 25 million people.

1384 The Bible is translated into English

1453 France wins the Hundred Years' War. England gives up its territory on the European mainland.

1066 Battle of Hastings—Normans beat the Anglo-Saxons to take control of the English throne

1180 First windmill built in Europe

1215 Magna Carta signed. The agreement limited the power of the English king.

1346 Battle of Crécy—English forces beat the French

1095–99 First Crusade

1449 Petrus Chritus paints *A Goldsmith in His Shop* (pp. 54–57)

1066   **1100**   **1200**   **1300**   **1400**

1202 First court jesters appear in Europe

1291 Crusades end with a Muslim victory

1415 Battle of Agincourt— The English defeat the French.

1456 Paolo Uccello paints *The Battle of San Romano* (pp. 34–37)

1337 Hundred Years' War begins— France and England fight a series of battles over territory

1073–1083 Bayeux Tapestry created (pp. 42–43)

1459 Jean Fouquet paints *Death of Clothar I* (pp. 8–11)

illuminated manuscript a book with pictures, written and painted by hand

joust a pretend fight between two knights on horseback. They gallop toward each other with lances and try to knock the opponent off his horse.

knight a fighting man who serves his lord or king when called upon to do so

lance a long, pointed wooden weapon used to knock an opponent off of a horse

lord a wealthy landowner who is often a knight as well

mace a club-like weapon with a sharp blade or spikes on the end

medieval from the Middle Ages

mortar a cement of clay, lime, and water

noble born into the highest social class (the nobility). Noble can also mean respectable.

oath a promise that is made before God or other witnesses

page a young boy who works for a knight

patron saint a saint who is believed to protect a certain place or group of people

rent money paid for the right to use something that is not yours, such as a house

siege an attack carried out by surrounding a town with an army, in an attempt to make the town give up control

squire a young man in training to become a knight

stag a male deer

steward an important servant in a castle who

organizes the work of other servants and looks after the money for the estate

stockade a fence made of sharpened wooden stakes

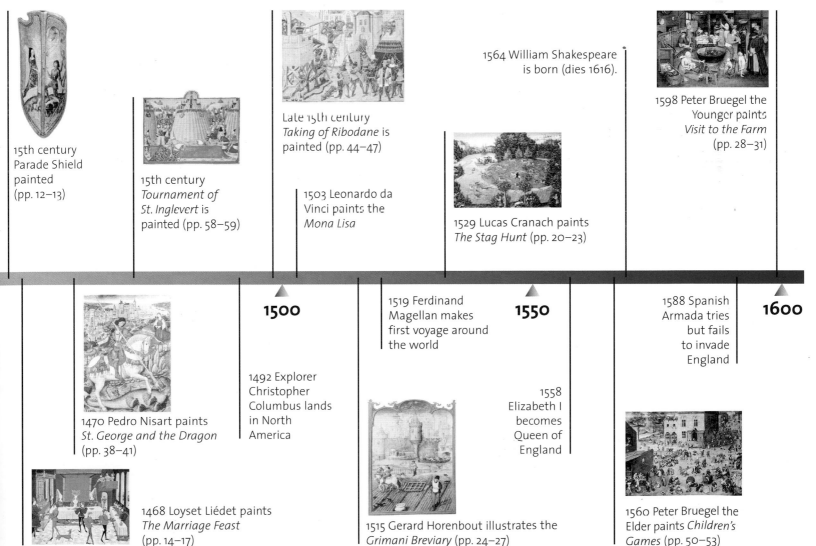

15th century Parade Shield painted (pp. 12–13)

15th century *Tournament of St. Inglevert* is painted (pp. 58–59)

Late 15th century *Taking of Ribodane* is painted (pp. 44–47)

1503 Leonardo da Vinci paints the *Mona Lisa*

1564 William Shakespeare is born (dies 1616).

1529 Lucas Cranach paints *The Stag Hunt* (pp. 20–23)

1598 Peter Bruegel the Younger paints *Visit to the Farm* (pp. 28–31)

1500

1519 Ferdinand Magellan makes first voyage around the world

1550

1588 Spanish Armada tries but fails to invade England

1600

1470 Pedro Nisart paints *St. George and the Dragon* (pp. 38–41)

1492 Explorer Christopher Columbus lands in North America

1558 Elizabeth I becomes Queen of England

1468 Loyset Liédet paints *The Marriage Feast* (pp. 14–17)

1515 Gerard Horenbout illustrates the *Grimani Breviary* (pp. 24–27)

1560 Peter Bruegel the Elder paints *Children's Games* (pp. 50–53)

Further Reading

Avi. *Crispin: The Cross of Lead.* New York: Hyperion, 2002.

Chrisp, Peter. *The Middle Ages.* My World series. Chanhassen, Minn.: Two-Can, 2002.

Deary, Terry. *The Measly Middle Ages.* New York: Scholastic, 1996.

Farman, John. *The Short and Bloody History of Knights.* Minneapolis: Lerner, 2003.

Gravett, Christopher. *Knight.* Eyewitness series. New York: Dorling Kindersley, 2000.

Howarth, Sarah. *What Do We Know about the Middle Ages?* New York: Peter Bedrick, 1995.

Langley, Andrew. *Medieval Life.* Eyewitness series. New York: Dorling Kindersley, 2000.

Macaulay, David. *Castle.* Boston: Houghton Mifflin, 1977.

McNeill, Sarah. *The Middle Ages.* New York: Oxford University Press, 1998.

Oakes, Catherine. *Exploring the Past: The Middle Ages.* San Diego: Harcourt, 1989.

Orme, Nicholas. *Medieval Children.* New Haven, Conn.: Yale University Press, 2001.

Platt, Richard. *Castle: Stephen Biesty's Cross-Sections.* New York: Dorling Kindersley, 1994.

Platt, Richard. *Castle Diary: The Journal of Tobias Burgess, Page.* Boston: Candlewick, 1999.

Websites

History of Medieval Europe
www.eyewitnesstohistory.com/mefrm.htm
History site with section on medieval history

http://www.learner.org/exhibits/middleages/
Information on all aspects of medieval life, written for children

www.medievalcrusades.com
History of the Crusades

www.historychannel.com

http://www.historyforkids.org

Castles
www.castles-of-britain.com

www.medieval-castles.net

Art of the Period
http://www.thebritishmuseum.ac.uk/compass/
Click on "Children's Compass" and check out the tours that use art from the British Museum to introduce children to subjects such as the Anglo-Saxons.

www.metmuseum.org
The Metropolitan Museum of Art, New York. Visit the page on The Cloisters for more information on the museum's collection of art from medieval Europe.

www.bayeuxtapestry.org.uk
This site explains in detail what is happening in each section of the Bayeux Tapestry.

Index

Picture Credits